Philosophy for children

From child to children

Once upon a time!

Look for someone who values you!

Coloring story!

By: Bernardo Octaviano Pereira

This book belongs to:

____

I dedicate this work, firstly, to my parents who I love so much, to my teachers, to my dear aunts and to all my friends, may God bless you all infinitely!

Bernardo Octaviano Pereira

05/04/2024

Once upon a time, in a place near here, a little boy complained to his dad that the kids on his street didn't like him very much,

Dad thought, thought and thought and looking at a corner of the yard, where he saw an old car, which they had not used for a long time.

So dad told the little boy that he should pick up and take that old car to the car fair near his house and see how much he could sell the car for.

So he did, he took the car and took him where his daddy had told him, when the little boy came home,

Dad asked how much they gave for the old car, and the little boy said that they didn't like his model and that they would give five hundred dollars.

Dad said, now you take him and take him to the dealership and ask how much he's worth, and the little boy went,

When the little boy came back, Dad asked how much he was worth, and he said that they would think he was very old and that he was worth about two thousand dollars,

And dad told him again that he should take her to an antique car exhibition and there he would research what its value would be, so he did.

When he came home, daddy asked the little boy how much he was worth, and the little boy said that everyone liked him and said he was unique,

a rarity, classic, that was a jewel on wheels and will offer ten thousand dollars.

Look how things are, said the father to the little boy, we have to go where we are valued and be with those who like us,

and not where we are devalued, we also have to be like this, go where we are valued and hang out with those who like us.

The end!